Samsung Gala (5G) User Manual for Beginners and Seniors

The Most Complete & Fascinating User Guide with Tips & Tricks, Coupled with Navigational Screenshots to Set up & Manipulate Tab A9

Tech World

Introduction

Within this comprehensive guide, you will find a wealth of information covering every aspect of your device, from its fundamental features to its more advanced functions. This will enable you to harness the full potential of your gadget.

By making use of convenient methods of communication like phone calls, messaging, and other helpful tools, it is possible to acquire the skill of effectively communicating with family and friends.

Furthermore, the contents of this book offer a novel and insightful perspective that will be highly beneficial to seasoned readers. Without a doubt, clicking the purchase button will be a choice that you will not lament.

Table of Contents

Device layout and functions

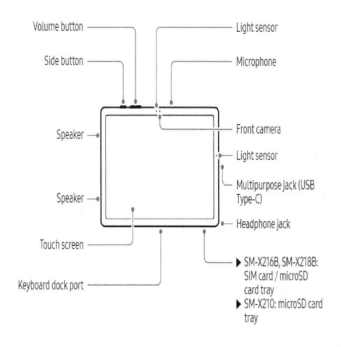

Volume button — Light sensor

Side button — Microphone

Speaker — Front camera

Light sensor

Multipurpose jack (USB Type-C)

Speaker — Headphone jack

Touch screen

▸ SM-X216B, SM-X218B: SIM card / microSD card tray
▸ SM-X210: microSD card tray

Keyboard dock port

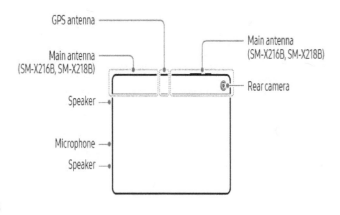

GPS antenna

Main antenna (SM-X216B, SM-X218B)

Main antenna (SM-X216B, SM-X218B)

Rear camera

Speaker

Microphone

Speaker

Chapter One
Turning the device on and off

In places like airlines and hospitals where using wireless devices is prohibited, it's important to heed all displayed warnings and recommendations from authorized employees.

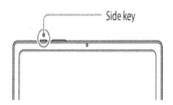

Turning the device on
Holding down the Side button for a few seconds will activate the device.

Turning the device off
1. Press and hold the Side key to power off the device. Alternative: swipe down to reveal the notification shade and press ⏻.

2. Tap power off.

   Select Restart to force a reboot.

Forcing restart

You can reset your smartphone by pressing and holding the Side key and the Volume Down key for longer than 7 seconds if it has frozen and become unresponsive.

Initial setup

When you initially switch on your device or after a factory reset, it will walk you through the setup process.

Note: Some functions of the device may not be configurable until after you have connected to a Wi-Fi network.

Samsung account

The Samsung services on your mobile device, TV, and the Samsung website are all accessible through your Samsung account, which is an integrated account service.

Visit account.samsung.com to see all the features compatible with your Samsung account.

1. Open Samsung account from the Settings menu.

Another option is to go the Settings menu and navigate to Accounts and backup > Manage accounts > Add account > Samsung account.

2. Log in with your existing Samsung account information.

- You may use your Google credentials to sign in by selecting Continue with Google.

- Create an account by selecting the option if you haven't already done so.

Finding your ID and resetting your password

On the Samsung account sign-in screen, you'll see options to Find ID or Forgot password? if you've lost track of either your Samsung account ID or password. After providing the requested details, you will be able to retrieve your ID and change your password.

Signing out of your Samsung account

Your personal information, including contacts and calendar events, will be deleted from your Samsung device after you check out of your account.

1. Open the Settings app and select Accounts and backup > Manage accounts.

2. Select Samsung account > My profile > Sign out.

3. Enter the password for your Samsung account and select OK to sign out.

Transfer data from your previous device via smart switch

Smart Switch allows you to easily move all of your data from your old device to your new one. Open the Accounts and backup section of Settings and select Bring data from old device.

Note: Some computers and gadgets may not be able to use this feature.

Exceptions are not made. For further information, please go to www.samsung.com/smartswitch.

Copyright is very important to Samsung. Don't send anything until you have the authority to send it.

Wireless data transfer

Use Wi-Fi Direct to wirelessly move information from your old device to your new one.

1. The first step is to open Smart Switch on the preceding device.

   You can get the app from the Galaxy Store or the Play Store if you don't already have it.

2. Open the Settings menu and then select Accounts and backup. Please provide your old device's data.

3. Put the gadgets in close proximity to one another.

4. Select Wireless from the preceding device and press Send data.

5. Tap Allow on the prior device.

6. Pick a transportable object on your device and then hit the Transfer button.

Using external storage to back up and restore data

Move information using a microSD card or other external storage device.

1. First, copy everything off of your old device into an external drive.

2. Connect or insert the external storage device.

3. Navigate to the Accounts and backup section of the Settings menu, and then select External storage transfer.

4. Under Restore from SD card, choose the backup date, and then tap Restore.

5. Copy files from an external device by following the on-screen prompts.

Copy backup data from a computer

Communicate your device's data to a PC. The Smart Switch app for computers is available for download at www.samsung.com/smartswitch. Transfer information from a computer backup to your new device.

1. To get Smart Switch for your PC, go to www.samsung.com/smartswitch.

2. Open Smart Switch in your PC.

   Note: If your old device isn't a Samsung, use the manufacturer-supplied software to transfer your data to a computer.

3. Use the USB cord to link your old gadget to the PC.

4. Transfer your data from the device to the computer by following the on-screen prompts.

   You must then remove the prior gadget from the computer.

5. Plug the USB cord into your computer and your device.

6. To copy files from your computer to your gadget, just follow the on-screen prompts.

Understanding the screen

Tapping

Tap the screen.

Tapping and holding

Tap and hold the screen for approximately 2 seconds.

Dragging

Tap and hold an item and drag it to the target position.

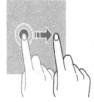

Double-tapping

Double-tap the screen.

Swiping

Swipe upwards, downwards, to the left, or to the right.

Spreading and pinching

Spread two fingers apart or pinch on the screen.

Precaution: Keep the touchscreen away from any other electronic gadgets. Touchscreens are vulnerable to damage from electrostatic discharges.

- Do not tap the touchscreen with a sharp object or press too hard on it with your fingers to keep it in working order.

- Avoid leaving any static images on the touchscreen for extended periods of time. This could cause ghosting or afterimages (screen burn-in).

Note: Touches made too close to the screen's borders, outside the touch input region, may be ignored by the device.

Navigation bar (soft buttons)

When the screen is turned on, the soft buttons show in the bottom navigation bar. By default, you can use the soft buttons to access the Recents menu, your home screen, and the previous menu. In different apps or in different contexts, the buttons' actions may shift.

Button		Function
|||	Recents	• Tap to open the list of recent apps.
○	Home	• Tap to return to the Home screen. • Tap and hold to launch the **Google Assistant** app.
〈	Back	• Tap to return to the previous screen.

Hiding the navigation bar

You can get a fuller view of your files or program by hiding the menu bar.

When the Settings menu appears, select Display > Navigation bar > Swipe gestures. When you use a gesture, the menu bar disappears and helpful instructions show. Select the desired choice by tapping the More button.

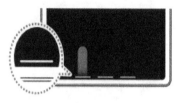

Swipe from bottom

Swipe from sides and bottom

Gesture hints can be turned off by tapping the corresponding button at the bottom of the screen.

Home screen and Apps screen

All of the functions of the smartphone can be accessed from the Home screen. There are widgets and app launchers on show.

Icons for all apps, including recently downloaded ones, may be found on the Apps screen.

Switching between Home and Apps screens

The Apps screen may be accessed from the Home screen by swiping up.

On the Apps screen, swiping up or down will take you back to the Home screen. The Home or Back buttons can also be used.

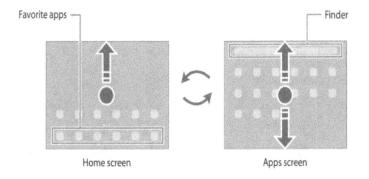

Favorite apps   Finder

Home screen   Apps screen

The Apps panel can be accessed by touching the Apps button, which can be added to the Home screen. To enable the Show Apps screen button on Home screen toggle, tap and hold an empty spot on the Home screen, select Settings, and then hit the appropriate button. At the very end of the Home screen, you'll find the new Apps button.

— Apps button

Editing the Home screen

To enter the editing menu, tap and hold an empty place on the Home screen, or pinch your fingers together. You have complete control over the background and gadgets. Panels on the Home screen can be moved, deleted, or added to in any way you like.

- Swipe left to access additional panels, and tap ⊕ to add them.

- To reposition a panel, tap and hold its preview until you see the repositioning icons, and then release.

- To remove a panel, tap on 🗑 .

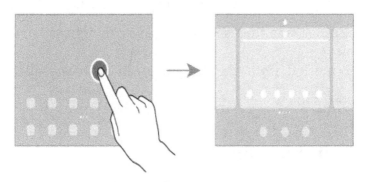

- Wallpaper: Allows you to customize the background image used both while the device is unlocked and when it is in use.

- Widgets: These mini-programs can be found on your Home screen and are used to access certain features within larger applications. Choose a gadget and hit the + button. The app's widget will be installed in the app's main menu.

- In the 'Settings' menu, you can alter the look and feel of the Home screen.

Displaying all apps on the home screen

You can configure your device such that all apps appear on the Home screen rather than on a dedicated Apps panel. Simply tap and hold an empty section of the Home screen, navigate to Settings, and then select Home screen only.

Swipe left from the Home screen to access all of your apps.

Launching finder

Quickly find what you're looking for on the smartphone.

1. Select Search from the Apps screen. Alternative: swipe down to reveal the notification shade and press Q.

2. Type in a search term.

    Your device's apps and data will be combed through.

    The keyboard can be used to look up additional information.

Moving items

Drag and drop an item by tapping and holding it down. Simply drag the item to the side of the screen to transfer it to a different panel.

Tap and hold an item in the Apps screen, and then select Add to Home to place a shortcut to that app on the Home screen. The app's icon will be placed in the app drawer. The bottom of the Home screen can be utilized to house commonly accessed app shortcuts.

Creating folders

Make use of folders to group apps of a similar nature for easy access and launch.

You can move one app onto another by tapping and holding it on the Home screen or the Apps screen.

The chosen programs will be placed in a new directory. Select Folder name and type in the folder's label.

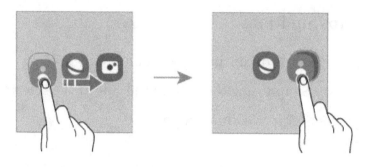

Adding more apps

Use your finger to select the folder. Select the programs you want to add, and then press the Done button. You can also drop an app into the designated folder.

Moving apps from a folder

Simply tap and hold an app to move it.

Deleting a folder

Select a folder by holding down the tap button, and then delete it. This action will only remove the folder. The contents of the folder will be moved to the Apps screen.

Edge panel

The Edge panels provide instant access to your most used apps and functionalities.

You can do this by bringing the Edge panel's handle into the middle of the screen.

If the Edge panel's toggle is hidden, open the Settings app, navigate to Display, and then hit the toggle for the panel.

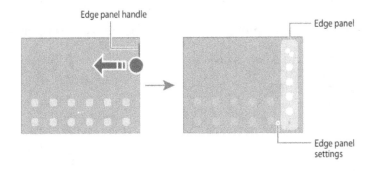

Lock screen

By pressing the Side button, you can lock and turn off the display. When the device hasn't been used for a while, it powers down and locks itself.

Swipe either direction after the screen lights up to unlock it.

If the display is dark, pressing the Side key will activate it. You can also double-tap the display.

Changing the screen lock method

Open the Settings app and navigate to Lock screen > Screen lock type to alter the screen lock mechanism.

Screen locks, whether they are patterns, PINs, passwords, or biometric data, allow you to restrict access to your device and thus your data. Once a screen lock mechanism has been selected, the device will always ask for a password or PIN to be unlocked.

Note: If you repeatedly enter the wrong unlock code and reach the maximum number of attempts allowed, your device can be programmed to erase all user data and return it to factory settings. Simply unlock the screen using the default screen lock mechanism, open the Settings menu, and toggle the "Auto factory reset" option on.

Indicator icons

The top of the screen displays a status bar with indicator icons. The most popular icons are shown in the table below.

Icon	Meaning
$\oslash$	No signal
.ıll	Signal strength
ᴿıll	Roaming (outside of normal service area)
G	GPRS network connected
E	EDGE network connected
3G	UMTS network connected
H	HSDPA network connected
H+	HSPA+ network connected

Icon	Meaning
4G / LTE	LTE network connected
📶	Wi-Fi connected
*	Bluetooth feature activated
📍	Location services being used
📞	Call in progress
⤻	Missed call
▣	New text or multimedia message
🔔	Alarm activated
🔇	Mute mode
✈	Airplane mode activated
⚠	Error occurred or caution required
🔋/🔋	Battery charging / Battery power level

Note: In some programs, the upper status bar might not show up at all. Simply pull down from the screen's top to reveal the status bar.

- Some icons for notifications only show up while the panel is open.

- Depending on your service provider or device model, the indication icons may look slightly different.

Notification panel

The status bar will update with fresh notification symbols as they come in. You can open the notification panel and read the descriptions of the icons there.

Simply pull the status bar to the bottom to reveal the alerts menu. Swipe up on the screen to hide the notification drawer.

The alert panel features the following options.

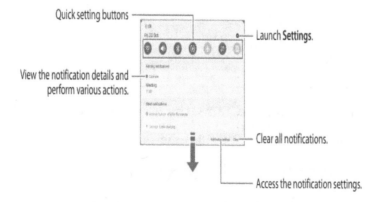

Quick setting buttons

Launch **Settings**.

View the notification details and perform various actions.

Clear all notifications.

Access the notification settings.

Using quick settings buttons

In order to engage a function, simply tap its shortcut button. To access additional options in the notification shade, swipe down. Tap⊕to add another button.

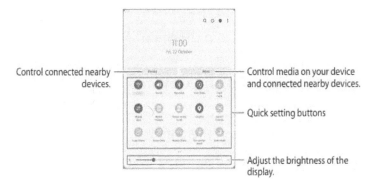

Tap the button's label to make adjustments to its settings, tap and hold a button to see granular configuration options.

Select ⋮ >Edit buttons, then tap and hold a button to move it, before releasing it in a new position.

Controlling media playback

Using Media, you can effortlessly manage your media playback. You can switch to a different device and keep listening from there.

1. Swipe down from the top of the screen to open the notification panel, and then tap Media.

2. Use the controller's buttons to skip songs, change the volume, and more.

   Select the device you'd want to continue playing on from the Smart View menu.

Controlling nearby devices

Quickly activate it and manage nearby connected devices straight from the panel of notifications.

1. Swipe down from the top of the screen to open the notification area, and then tap Devices.

   You'll be able to see the nearby connected gadgets.

2. Pick a nearby device to use as a remote.

Screen capture and screen record

Screen capture

Take a screenshot on the go and edit, annotate, or share the resulting image in any way you see fit. The current window and its scrollable contents can be saved.

How to capture a screenshot

Take a screenshot by following these steps. Gallery is where you may check out those screenshots you took.

Method 1: grab keys by simultaneously pressing the Side and Volume Down buttons.

Method 2: Capture with a swipe of your palm to the left or right across the display.

Note: Some programs and functions prevent you from taking a screenshot.

- Launch the Settings app, navigate to Advanced features > Motions & gestures, and toggle the Palm swipe to capture switch on if it is not already.

After taking a screenshot, you can edit it using the buttons at the screen's bottom.

- ⌜⌄⌟: To record both the visible and invisible information on a long page (like a website). When you tap ⌜⌄⌟ and hold down, the screen will scroll down to capture additional content.

- ⌁: You can annotate the snapshot by writing or drawing on it, or by cutting out a specific area. Gallery displays the area that was cut out.

- ⌁: Distribute the captured image to your friends.

Note: If the toggle for the Screenshot toolbar isn't already on when you take a screenshot, open the Settings app, navigate to Advanced features, and then select Screenshots and screen recorder.

Screen record
Capture the action on your screen while you work.

1. Open the notification shade by swiping down from the top of the screen; then, hit ⊙ (Screen recorder).

2. Pick a recording mode and hit the record button. There will be a countdown before recording begins.

- You can use the on screen keyboard by tapping 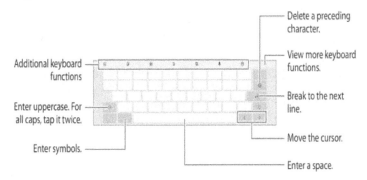.

3. Tap the stop button ■ when you're done recording.

   Gallery is where you can watch the clip.

Note: Launch the Settings app and navigate to Advanced features Screenshots and screen recorder to modify the screen recorder settings.

Entering text

Keyboard layout
When you start typing, the computer brings up a keyboard.

Note: Some languages don't allow for text input. You can't enter text until you select a language from the list of those that can do so.

Changing the input language

Select the languages you'd like to use by tapping Languages and types Manage input languages. The input languages can be changed by swiping left or right on the space bar or by clicking ⊕.

Changing the keyboard

You can switch keyboard layouts by tapping ⌨ on the navigation bar.

Select the desired keyboard layout by tapping ⚙ > Languages and types, then choosing the desired language.

Note: If the keyboard icon (⌨) is not present on the toolbar, you can enable it by opening the Settings app, going to General management, and then Keyboard list and default.

Additional keyboard functions

- ☺ : Enter emojis.
- 🙂 : Enter stickers.
- [GIF] : Attach animated GIFs.
- 🖉 : Switch to handwriting mode.
- ⌨ : Change the keyboard mode.
- 🎤 : Enter text by voice.
- ⚙ : Change the keyboard settings.

Tap ••• to use more keyboard functions.

- Q : Search for content and enter it.
- 🗛 : Translate text and enter it.
- 📋 : Add an item from the clipboard.
- ⟨⟩ : Open the text editing panel.
- 🔲 : Change the keyboard size.

Note: Depending on your service provider or device model, some features may be disabled.

Copying and pasting

1. Click and hold the text.

2. Select the text you want by dragging 🔵 or 🔵 , or use the Select all button.

3. In just three taps, you can copy or cut anything.

When you copy text, it goes straight to your clipboard.

4. Select the desired location to paste the text and then hit the Paste button.

You can paste copied text by selecting it and then using the Clipboard button.

Chapter Two
Apps and features

Galaxy store

Get app-buying and getting done. There are apps available for download that are designed specifically for Samsung Galaxy handsets.

Start up the Galaxy Store program. Check out the app selection by browsing categories or using the Q search bar.

Note: The availability of this app is service provider and device specific.

- To modify the settings for automatic app updates, go to Settings > ≡ > ⚙ >Auto update applications.

Play store

Get app-buying and getting done.

Open the Google Play app. Downloadable apps can be explored in a variety of ways.

Note: After tapping the account icon, following the path Settings > Network options > Auto-update apps, and finally making your choice.

Uninstalling or disabling apps

Select a menu item by tapping and holding an app.

- In order to remove previously installed software, use the "Uninstall" button.

- If an app is installed by default and cannot be removed, you can disable it using the disable option.

Note: This functionality may not be available in all apps.

Enabling apps

To enable an app, open Settings, go to Apps, then press ⌷ > Disabled, and then OK.

Setting app permissions

Some apps may require access to or usage of information on your smartphone in order to function effectively.

Settings Apps will show you the current permissions for each installed app, choose an app, and then go to Settings. The app's permissions can be seen and modified.

Launch the Settings app, then navigate to Apps >⋮> Permission manager to view or modify app permission settings by permission category. Choose an action and then pick a program.

Note: It's possible that even the most fundamental software functionalities won't work if you refuse to provide permissions to them.

Chapter Three
Phone

Participate in or respond to a video or audio call.

Note: The Call & text on other devices switch must be activated in the Settings app, under "Advanced features," before you may make calls or send texts from other devices. To sync your devices, you'll need to create and use the same Samsung account on each of them. There could be gaps in the functionality of calls and messages.

Making calls

1. Open the Phone app and select Keypad.

2. Put in a phone number.

3. Three taps connect you for a voice call; four taps launch a video call.

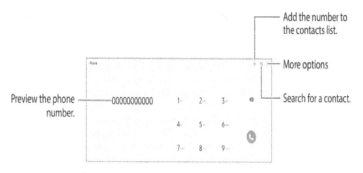

Add the number to the contacts list.

More options

Preview the phone number.

Search for a contact.

Making calls from call logs or contact list

To dial a number or contact, open the Phone app, go to Recents or Contacts, and then swipe right.

To enable Swipe to call or text, go to options ⁝ > Settings > Other call options and toggle the switch on.

Using speed dial

Starting the Phone app, tapping Keypad or Contacts >⁝>Speed dial numbers, choosing a speed dial number, and adding a phone number are the steps to adding a number to speed dial.

Simply press and hold a speed dial number on the keyboard to place a call. Tap the initial digit(s) of the number, then tap and hold the last digit to make a speed dial.

To create the speed dial 123, for instance, you would hit 1, then tap 2, and then tap and hold 3.

Making an international call

1. Open the Phone app and select Keypad.

2. Press and hold the zero key until the plus symbol appears.

3. Dial the international access code, local area code, and phone number.

Receiving calls

Picking up the phone

To answer a call, simply drag ☎ outside the main circle.

Rejecting a call

To answer a call, simply ☎ drag outside the main circle.

When rejecting a call, you can choose to send a message instead of just hanging up by dragging the Send message bar up and clicking the desired message.

Quick refuse messages can be customized in the Phone settings by opening the app, tapping ⋮ > Settings > Quick decline messages, entering a custom message, and then tapping ＋.

Blocking phone numbers

Prevent incoming calls from numbers you specify.

1. Open Phone, go to Settings, and then tap Block numbers.

2. Select the desired contacts or phone numbers from Recents or Contacts, and then select Done. If you want to input a number manually, select Add phone number, type in the number, and then select ╉.

You will not be notified of any attempts to contact you from blacklisted numbers. The call history will be recorded.

Note: In addition, you can prevent calls from reaching you from unknown numbers by blocking them. To use this function, you must toggle the switch labeled "Block unknown/private numbers."

Options during calls

- It's possible to make a second call by selecting the "Add call" option. The first call is going to be placed on hold. When you hang up, your initial call will automatically reconnect.

- Message: Lets you leave a voicemail for the caller.

- If a Bluetooth headset is available, switch to using that.

- Hold call pauses an incoming call.

- To prevent the other party from hearing you, press the mute button.

- To use the keypad, open it. Simply tapping ⌄ will close the keypad.

- ☎ : Hang up the phone now.

- To avoid being seen on a video conference, you should disable your camera.

- You may toggle between the front and back cameras during a call.

Note: Depending on your service provider or device model, some features may be disabled.

Chapter Four
Contacts

Make new contacts or manage existing ones.

Adding contacts

1. Open up your phone's Contacts app and tap ✛.

2. Decide on a storage facility.

3. Fill up your details and hit Save.

Importing contacts

Import your existing contact list into your device.

1. Open Contacts, then hit ☰ > Manage > Import or export contacts > Import.

2. Import contacts by following the on-screen prompts.

Syncing contacts with your web accounts

You can synchronize your Samsung account's contacts with those stored on your mobile device.

1. Open the Settings app, navigate to Accounts and backup, and then press Manage accounts.

2. Initiate the Contacts sync by tapping the Sync account and Contacts switch.

Search for contacts

Bring up the Contacts program. Select the $\mathcal{Q}$ search bar at the top of the contacts list and type in your criteria.

Select the contact and tap on it. Then, do something like this:

Deleting contacts

1. Open the Contacts app, touch ⋮ > Delete contacts button at the top of the contacts list.

2. Pick certain contacts and hit the Delete button.

   To remove a contact individually, tap their name in the contacts list, then select More > Delete.

Sharing contacts

Several methods exist for disseminating your contact list to those around you.

1. Open the Contacts app by tapping the icon ⋮ in the upper right corner of your screen.

2. The second step is to pick some friends to share with.

3. Decide on a means of communication to spread the news.

Creating groups

Groups can be created, such as those for family and friends, and contacts can be organized accordingly.

1. Start up your Contacts app and click ☰ > Groups > Create group.

2. The second step is to form a group by following the on screen prompts.

Merging duplicate contacts

If you have multiple entries for the same person in your contact list, merge them into a single entry.

1. Open up Contacts, then select ☰ > Manage contacts, > Merge contacts or anything similar.

2. To merge two lists, choose the contacts.

Messages

View and respond to messages in a threaded format.

Messages sent or received while roaming may attract additional fees.

Note: The Call & text on other devices switch must be activated in the Settings app, under "Advanced features," before you may make calls or send texts from other devices. To sync your devices, you'll need to create and use the same Samsung account on each of them. There could be gaps in the functionality of calls and messages.

Sending messages

1. Hit Messages app to open it and touch ✛.

2. Type in a message and add some recipients. Simply tap and hold, utter your message, and then release your finger to send a recorded voice message. Only when there is no text in the input box does the recording symbol appear.

3. Just tap ◐ to deliver your message.

Recipient — Enter recipients.

Enter a message. — Enter stickers.

Attach files. — Send the message.

Viewing messages

1. Open up the Messages program.

2. Choose a person or a number from the list of recipients in your messages.

- Tap the message input field, type your response, and then tap  to send it.

- For larger or smaller text, spread your fingers or pinch the screen.

Sorting messages

Messages can be organized and managed based on their respective categories.

To do this, open Messages, then go to Conversations and add a new category.

To enable categories for conversations, hit ⋮ > Settings and toggle Conversations categories on.

Deleting messages

To erase a message, tap and hold it before selecting erase.

Changing message settings

Open Messages and then select ⋮ > Settings from the menu. You have the option of blocking undesirable messages and modifying your notification preferences.

Internet

Search the web for what you need, and save links to useful sites so you can quickly return to them.

1. Open your web browser.

2. Type in the URL or search term, and then press the Go button.

   You may access the menu bars by swiping your finger down on the screen.

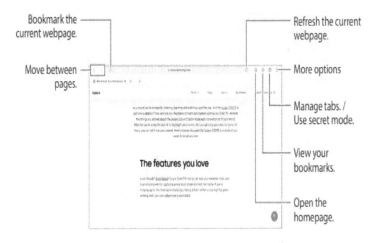

Using secret mode

By activating a password-protected "secret mode," you can shield your private data from prying eyes.

1. Click ⬜ >Switch on Secret mode.

2. Activate secret mode by tapping the Lock Secret mode option, then hit Start and enter a password.

   When in stealth mode, the gadget's toolbars will take on a different hue. Tap 🗗 >Turn off Secret mode to disable stealth mode.

Note: Some functions, such screen capturing, are disabled while in stealth mode.

Chapter Five
Camera

Make use of a number of camera and video recording modes and settings.

Camera etiquette

- Avoid taking images or videos of other individuals without their knowledge or consent.

- Do not photograph or film in restricted areas.

- Don't snap photos or make recordings in situations where you might infringe on the privacy of others.

Taking pictures

1. Start up the camera program.

   Pressing the Side key twice as fast will open the app, as will swiping left on the locked screen.

Note: If you run the Camera app while the screen is locked, or if you switch off the screen while the screen lock method is active, you will not have access to all of the camera's functions.

- When not in use, the camera powers down.

- Depending on your service provider or device model, you may not have access to all accessible methods.

2. Select the area of the preview screen where you want the camera to focus by tapping there.

   Slide the bar that appears above or below the circular frame to change the image's brightness.

3. Take a picture with three taps.

   You can switch shooting modes by swiping the preview screen or dragging the shooting modes list to the left or right.

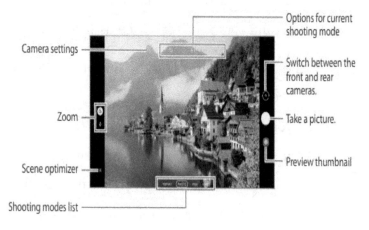

Options for current shooting mode

Camera settings

Switch between the front and rear cameras.

Zoom

Take a picture.

Scene optimizer

Preview thumbnail

Shooting modes list

Note: Depending on the camera model and shooting mode, the preview screen may seem different.

- If your subject is far away, the focus may not be clear in high-resolution or high-zoom ratio photographs or movies. Get a far distance and shoot stills or video.

- Clear the lens of the camera and try again if your photos come out fuzzy.

- Verify that the lens is clean and undamaged. Some modes that make use of the device's high resolutions may not function properly if that resolution is not met.

- The camera on your device has a wide-angle lens. Taking a wide-angle photo or video may result in some little distortion, but this is not indicative of any performance issues with your device.

- The maximum recording capacity of a video camera may change with the video's resolution.

- Due to the temperature difference between the outside and interior of the camera cover, the camera may fog up or create condensation if the device is exposed to abrupt variations in air temperature. If you can, avoid taking photos in direct sunlight. If your camera fogs up, it's best to let it dry out at room temperature before snapping photos or shooting video.

Using zoom features

To zoom in or out, click ⌗ / ⌗ and drag the zoom bar. As an alternative, you can use the space between your fingers to zoom in, and a pinch to zoom out.

- ⌗ : Make standard photographs or video recordings.

- ⌗ : Capture images or video by zooming in on the topic.

Note: The front-facing camera lacks zoom capabilities.

Locking the focus (AF) and exposure (AE)

To prevent the camera from making adjustments in response to changes in the foreground or background, you can lock the focus or exposure on a particular area.

Focus and exposure can be locked by tapping and holding the desired region; the AF/AE frame will then show over the tap target. Even after you take a picture, you can't change the settings.

Note: Depending on the shooting mode, this function may be unavailable.

Using the camera button

- To start recording a video, tap and hold the camera button.

- Swipe the camera button to the edge of the screen and hold it to snap multiple images at once.

- If you add a second camera button, you can put it wherever on the display for easier access. To use the Floating Shutter button,

toggle it on in the preview screen under ⚙ >
Shooting Modes.

Options for current shooting mode

Here are some choices you can make on the preview
screen.

- ⚡ : Toggle the flash on/off switch.

- ⏱OFF : Set the time elapsed before the camera
  takes a picture automatically.

- 3:4 : Pick a picture aspect ratio.

- 8x : Please choose a frame rate above.

- 9:16 : Video aspect ratio must be set.

- FHD 30 : Pick a resolution for recording video.

- ✨: Use a filter or some other cosmetic
  enhancements.

- ◎: Decide on a metering strategy. How
  luminous intensity is determined depends on
  this. The exposure in a ◎ center-weighted
  photograph is based on the amount of

available light in the image's center. (o) Spot determines exposure based on the amount of light in the image's focal plane. (◊) Matrix takes an average of the whole room.

- ○ : In FOOD mode, you should zoom in on a certain area inside the circular frame and blur the surrounding area.

- ⊕ : Change the hue in the FOOD setting.

Note: Model and shooting mode can affect the available settings.

Photo modes

The camera's shooting options are instantly adjusted to the current environment, making it simple to take photos.

Select PHOTO from the list of available shooting modes.

Scene optimizer

When the camera identifies its subject, a new option appears on the scene optimizer button, allowing you to select the most appropriate color and effect.

Note: If you want to use this function, make sure it's turned on by tapping the Scene optimizer option in the preview screen.

Taking selfies

The front-facing camera allows for self-portraiture.

1. One can take a self-portrait by swiping up or down on the preview screen to activate the front-facing camera or tap ⊙.

2. Present one's front to the camera.

   Tap ⊕ to take a wide-angle selfie of yourself in front of a scenic backdrop or a group of friends.

3. Take a picture with three taps ◯.

Applying filter and beauty effects

Before snapping a photo, you can adjust your skin tone and face shape, as well as apply a filter effect.

1. Tap ✳ the on the preview screen.

2. Decide on some filters, and snap a shot.

Video mode

The camera's shooting options adapt mechanically to the conditions, making it simple to capture moving pictures.

1. To start recording a video, go to the shooting modes menu and select VIDEO and tap ⦿. Capturing a screenshot while recording is easy by tapping ▣.

2. Tap ⦿ the screen twice to end the recording.

Pro mode

Take images while you fiddle with the exposure and ISO settings manually.

Select MORE PRO from the list of shooting modes. Tap the shutter button after making your selections and adjusting the parameters and tap ◯.

Available options:

- ISO : Decide on an ISO setting. Light sensitivity of the camera can be adjusted here. Values near zero indicate inanimate or well-lit subjects. Objects in motion or in low light require higher values. However, images with a higher ISO setting may exhibit noise.

- WB : Set the white balance properly to capture the world as it really is. The color temperature can be adjusted.

- : Alter the amount of light permitted in. The amount of light reaching the camera's sensor is controlled by this. Increase the exposure time when working in dim conditions.

Panorama mode

To create a large scene, snap a sequence of photos in panorama mode and then stitch them together.

1. Select MORE > PANORAMA from the list of available shooting modes. Tap twice and carefully nudge the gadget in one way.

2. Make sure the subject stays within the confines of the viewfinder. The camera will automatically stop taking images if the preview image moves outside the guidance frame or if you do not move the device.

3. With three taps ■ , you can halt the camera's capture of images.

Note: Don't take photos against a blurry background like a cloudless sky or a blank wall.

Food mode
Add more color to your food photos.

1. Select MORE > FOOD from the list of available shooting modes. Highlight an area by tapping and dragging the circular frame.

2. Blurring will occur in the areas outside the circular frame.

   Drag a corner of the circular frame to resize it.

3. Modify the color saturation by tapping ⊕ and dragging the slider.

4. Tap ◯ to snap a photo.

Portrait mode

Use a blurred background to draw attention to the subject's face in your photographs.

1. First, select PORTRAIT from the list of available shooting modes.

2. Background blur can be adjusted by dragging the blur slider.

3. Tap the camera icon ◯ when the Effect Ready message displays in the preview.

Background blur adjustment bar —

Note

- Make sure there's enough light where you are before using this function.

- It's possible that the blurred background wasn't applied correctly due to:

- The machine or the thing being measured is in motion.

- The hue of the topic blends in with the background.

Hyper lapse mode

Fast-motion videos can be viewed by recording scenes and then watching them later.

1. Select MORE > HYPERLAPSE from the list of available shooting modes.

2. Tap ⌣ to choose a frame rate.

3. Tap ⬤ will begin the recording.

4. Hit ⬤ to halt recording.

Deco Pic mode

Take photos or movies while using a wide variety of stickers.

Select MORE > Deco Pic from the selection of shooting modes.

Customizing camera settings

To access the preview, press⚙. Depending on the shooting mode, you may not have access to all of the menu options.

Intelligent features

- Use the scene optimizer to have the device automatically alter the color settings and apply the optimized effect based on the scene or subject.

- You can use the smartphone to scan QR codes by enabling the feature on the preview screen.

Pictures

- Select an action to be carried out when the shutter button is swiped to the edge of the screen and held.

Selfies

- The device can be programmed to take a wide-angle selfie if more than two individuals are detected in the frame, making it ideal for group selfies.

- Set the device to save front-facing camera photos without rotating them as they appear in the preview screen.

Useful features

- With Auto HDR, your photos will have vivid colors and accurate details in both bright and dark settings.

- Grid lines provide compositional aid when choosing subjects and are displayed as viewfinder guides.

- Location tags: Label an image with its precise location using GPS.

  Note: In low-lying places, between buildings, or during inclement weather, the strength of a GPS signal may be diminished.

  – When you upload photos to the web, your location data may be visible to others. Turning off location tracking can help.

- Additional shooting modes can be selected for use when photographing or filming.

- When you turn the camera on, it will remember your previous settings, including the shooting mode.

- Choose where in memory you want your data saved. When a memory card is inserted, this option will become available.

- Watermark: Place a watermark in the image's bottom left corner.

- The shutter sound can be activated or deactivated here.

- Camera settings can be cleared by using the "Reset" button.

- Visit our contact page to submit a question or peruse our FAQ.

- Under "About Camera," you may check out the app's version and read the fine print.

Note: Depending on the version, not all advertised functions may be included.

Gallery

Check out the media files you've got stashed away. Photos and videos can be organized in albums, and narratives can be made.

Using gallery

Invoke the Gallery program.

More options

Search for images.

Viewing images

Bring up a picture in the Gallery software. Swipe the screen left or right to navigate between different documents.

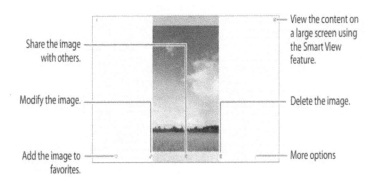

Share the image with others.

Modify the image.

Add the image to favorites.

View the content on a large screen using the Smart View feature.

Delete the image.

More options

Cropping enlarged images

1. Open Gallery and pick an existing image.

2. Place two fingers far apart on the screen and tap the area you wish to save and hit ⊞.

   A new file will be created containing only the clipped portion.

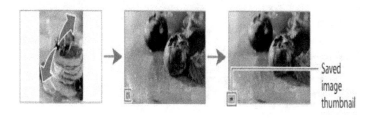

Saved
image
thumbnail

Viewing videos

Bring up a video in the Gallery app. Swipe the screen left or right to navigate between different documents.

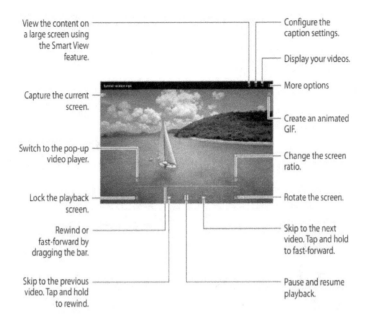

View the content on a large screen using the Smart View feature.

Configure the caption settings.

Display your videos.

More options

Capture the current screen.

Create an animated GIF.

Switch to the pop-up video player.

Change the screen ratio.

Lock the playback screen.

Rotate the screen.

Rewind or fast-forward by dragging the bar.

Skip to the next video. Tap and hold to fast-forward.

Skip to the previous video. Tap and hold to rewind.

Pause and resume playback.

To change the brightness, swipe your finger up or down the left side of the screen, and to change the volume, swipe your finger up or down the right side of the screen.

Swipe the playback screen to the left or right to rewind or skip ahead.

Albums

Make albums to organize your video and photo collections.

1. To begin making an album, open the Gallery app and select ☰ > Albums > ⋮ > Create album.

2. Pick the album you want to add to, then press the Add items button and drag and drop the media files you wish to include.

Stories

The device can read the time and place stamps on photos and videos you take or save, then arrange them into narratives.

Open the Gallery app and choose a tale by tapping ☰ >Stories.

Select a story and then tap ⋮ > Add or Edit to upload, remove, or edit media.

Deleting images or videos

To delete a photo, video, or narrative, open the Gallery app, tap and hold the item you want to remove, and then tap Delete.

Using the trash feature

Put the photos and videos you don't want any longer in the garbage. The data will be removed from storage at some point in the future.

Bring up the Gallery menu by pressing ≡ > ⚙ and then toggle the Trash button on and off.

Launch the Gallery app and select ≡ >Trash to see the trashed items.

Multi window

With multi-window, you can use the split-screen mode to use two applications at once. The pop-up window also allows you to use numerous applications simultaneously.

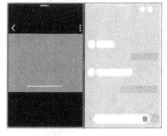
Split screen view

Pop-up view

Split screen view

1. Select Recently Used from the menu that appears.

2. Select an app by swiping left or right, tapping its icon, and then selecting Open in split-screen mode.

3. Pick a different app to run from the available options in the app list.

Launching apps from the Edge panel

1. First, while using an app, bring the Edge panel's control bar toward the middle of the display.

2. Select an app with two fingers, drag it to the left, and release it in the area labeled Drop here to open.

   When you choose an app, a split-screen mode will open.

Note: You can assign a single tap to open an app in the split-screen mode. To open in a split-screen mode, hit ☰ > Edit > ⋮ > and then click **Tap**. When the Show recent apps toggle is flipped on, the most recently used apps can be launched in a split-screen mode directly from the Edge panel.

Adding app pairs

Easily switch between two apps in a split-screen mode with just one press by adding them to the Edge panel.

1. First, when in split-screen mode, tap the circles to swap the positions of the app windows.

2. Tap ⊞.

    You can save the current app pair that you're using in split-screen mode on the Edge panel.

Adjusting the window size

To resize the app windows, simply drag the circles between them.

You can maximize a window by dragging its circle borders to the screen's edge.

Pop up view

1. Select Recently Used from the menu that appears.

2. Select an app by swiping left or right, tapping its icon, and finally selecting Open in pop-up view.

   The pop-up window will display the app's main screen.

   If you have a pop-up window open and you press the Home button, the window will be minimized and shown as an app icon. Repeatedly tapping the program icon brings up the pop-up window.

Launching apps from the Edge panel

1. Bring the Edge panel's control bar toward the middle of the display.

2. Select an app with two fingers, slide it to the left, and release it where it says Drop here for pop-up view.

   A new window will open up, showing the chosen program.

Moving pop-up windows

A pop-up window can be repositioned by tapping and dragging its title bar.

Samsung Notes

Enter text into a note using the keyboard, or handwrite or draw on the screen. Your notes can also include media like pictures and audio recordings.

Creating notes

1. Open the Samsung Notes app, select New Note, and enter the note's details.

   To switch the keyboard layout, select this icon or .

2. When you're done writing, hit the Back button to save the note. You can choose a different file type when you tap **⋮** > Save as file to store the note.

Deleting notes

To get rid of a note, tap and hold it, then select Delete.

Samsung members

Samsung Members provides consumers with access to technical help, including device problem diagnosis, as well as the ability to submit inquiries and bug reports. You may also check out the most recent news and hints, as well as interact with other Galaxy users. If you have any issues with your Samsung device, you can get in touch with other Samsung Members for assistance.

Galaxy shop

Visit Samsung's official site to learn more about their offerings.

Get the Galaxy Store app going.

Calendar

Plan ahead by writing down commitments and due dates in a planner.

Creating events

1. Select a date in the Calendar app by tapping ✛ or double-tapping it.

    If the date contains events or tasks saved to it, press the date and then tap ✛.

2. Save your event information.

Syncing events with your accounts

1. Open the Settings app, navigate to Accounts and backup, and then tap Manage accounts to choose the account you want to sync with.

2. Activate Calendar by tapping the Sync account and Calendar switch.

    Launch the Calendar app, and then select ≡ > ⚙ > Manage > calendars > ✛ to add accounts to sync with. Next, choose a sync destination and log in. A blue dot will appear

85

next to the account's name once it has been added.

Reminder

Log tasks as reminders and get alerts when they become due based on your own criteria.

Note: Connecting to a Wi-Fi or mobile network will improve the precision of your alerts.

- The GPS function must be enabled before the location reminders feature may be used. Depending on the device, you may not have access to location-based reminders.

Starting reminder

To set a reminder, open Calendar and press ≡ > Reminder. The Apps screen will update to include the Reminder app icon ( ), and the Reminder screen will load.

Creating reminders

1. Open up the Reminder program.

2. Select ✛ , fill in the information, and select Save.

Completing reminders

Hit ⬭ or select a reminder from the list and then hit Complete to finish it.

Restoring reminders

Restore finished reminders to their original status.

1. Select ☰ > Completed from the list of reminders.

2. Choose a backup reminder and hit the Restore button.

    You will be reminded once more, and reminder will be added to the list of reminders.

Deleting reminders

Select the reminder you want to remove and then click the Delete button. Hold down on a reminder, select the ones you want to get rid of, and then hit Delete.

Voice Recorder

Make or listen to a recording of your voice.

1. Start up the Voice Recorder program. Just tap on the screen twice to begin. Use the microphone, please.

- You can stop recording with a tap ⏸ .

- During the recording process, you can insert a bookmark by pressing the BOOKMARK button.

2. The recording will end after tapping ■ .

3. Pick a save name and hit the save button.

My Files

Use the device's storage to read and manipulate a wide range of files.

Bring up the My Files program.

Select Analyze storage to find duplicate or unused files and save up space on your device. To look for a certain folder or file, tap $\mathcal{Q}$.

Clock

You can use it to time an event or set an alarm, as well as to see what time it is in a variety of cities throughout the world. Open the Clock program.

Sharing content

Use a variety of sharing methods to disseminate information. What follows is a sample of image sharing.

1. Bring up your pictures in the Gallery app.

2. Tap ⌁ and choose the appropriate sharing option.

Note: Transferring data through a mobile network could result in additional fees.

Sharing content with nearby devices

Send data to adjacent devices using Wi-Fi Direct or Bluetooth, or to other gadgets that are Smart Things compatible.

1. Open Gallery and pick an existing image.

2. To activate ⊚ (Quick Share) on the other smartphone, open the notification panel, slide down from the top, and then tap. To include ⊚ (Quick Share) on your fast panel, simply tap ⊕ and drag the button there.

3. Select a device from the menu that appears when you tap ⤜ > Quick Share.

4. Allow the other device to complete the file transmission.

Note: Videos cannot be shared with TVs or other SmartThings-compatible devices at this time. Use the Smart View function to watch videos on your TV.

Setting who can find your device

Limit who can use your device and send you content.

1. To enable ⊚ (Quick Share), open the notification panel by swiping down from the top of the screen.

2. Two-finger tap and hold ⊚ (quick share). The Quick Share preferences window will show up.

3. Make a decision.

- Contacts only: Only those in my contact list who also have a Samsung mobile can view and send me files.

- Everybody: Let all the other gadgets around you access yours.

Smart View

Connect your mobile device to a TV or monitor that supports screen mirroring to view its display on a larger screen.

1. Swipe down from the top of the screen to open the notification shade, and then touch ⊚ (Smart View).

2. Choose an output device to reflect your screen.

Note: Smart View videos can be played at a variety of resolutions, depending on the TV model.

Samsung Flow

Samsung Flow makes it simple to link your tablet and phone for streamlined use, like viewing notifications and sharing media.

Both devices must have Samsung Flow installed for the connection to work. You can get Samsung Flow from the Galaxy Store or the Google Play Store if you don't already have it.

Note: Only few Samsung Android devices support this functionality.

- The Bluetooth function on both the tablet and the phone must be enabled for use of this feature.

Connecting your tablet and smartphone

1. Open Samsung Flow on your mobile device.

2. Start the Samsung Flow app on your tablet computer.

3. The next step is to choose your smartphone from the list of recognized devices.

4. Allow the other device to connect to yours.

5. Verify the password on both devices in step

All the gadgets will be linked together.

Note: If your smartphone has a fingerprint reader, you can use Samsung Pass to connect devices quickly and safely with only a touch of your finger.

Checking notification on your tablet

If your smartphone alerts you to new notifications, you can view them on your tablet by selecting **NOTIFICATIONS**.

Sharing contents

The information on your smartphone can be transferred to your tablet.

Samsung TV plus

Just like a regular TV, you may flip between the stations to watch a wide variety of shows and movies completely for free. Fire up the Samsung TV Plus software.

Note: Depending on your network provider and device, this app might not be a viable option.

Google apps

Google's app store includes games, social networking, and productivity tools. Some apps may ask you to sign in with your Google account.

Check out the app's respective help section for further details.

- Chrome can be used to look for data and navigate the web.

- Use Google's email service, Gmail, to communicate electronically.

- Maps: locate your current position, look for a specific location anywhere in the world, and examine maps of neighboring areas.

- YT Music: Watch music videos and listen to music on YouTube. The music libraries you've saved on your device can be accessed and played as well.

- Videos like movies and TV shows can be bought or rented from the Play Store section of Google Play.

- Drive is a cloud storage and file sharing service that allows you to view your files from any internet-connected device.

- You may watch videos, upload your own, and share them with others on YouTube.

- Photos allow you to find, organize, and modify images and videos across several devices.

- Google lets you conduct a rapid search of the web or your mobile device.

- Make a quick video call with Duo.

- Messages: Communicate with other users by text message or email, and share media files like photos and videos.

Note: Depending on your network provider or device model, not all apps may be accessible.

Settings

Modify the system to your liking. Open the system preferences menu.

To conduct a keyword search of the configurations, select $\mathcal{Q}$. Choose a tag under Suggestions to narrow your search for a certain configuration.

Samsung account

To take charge of your Samsung account, just log in. Samsung account may be accessed from the Settings menu.

Connections

Modify settings for wireless and wired networks including Wi-Fi and Bluetooth.

Select Connections from the Settings menu.

- Wi-Fi: To access the web or other networked devices, you can turn on the Wi-Fi function by connecting to a wireless network.

- Bluetooth: In order to share information or media files with other Bluetooth-enabled devices, you can make use of Bluetooth. If you need further information, check out Bluetooth.

- Airplane mode: By activating the device's airplane mode, you can prevent any wireless connections from being made or received. Only non-network services will be available to you.

  Precaution: Please abide by the airline's rules and the instructions of flight attendants. always put your phone or other mobile device into airplane mode when flying.

- Mobile networks: Set up your network preferences.

- Data usage: Limit your monthly data transfer by entering a specific amount. Limit your usage of mobile data by having the device cut off the connection automatically when you hit your limit.

  Data saving mode can be used to stop some background programs from sending or receiving data. For further info, see out Data saver (models compatible with mobile networks).

  Even when your device is linked to a Wi-Fi network, you have the option of designating certain apps to always use mobile data. For more info on mobile network capable models, check our mobile data only apps.

- Tethering and mobile hotspot: Allows you to share your mobile data connection with other devices. Refer to Mobile Hotspot (Mobile network equipped models) for further details regarding the portable wireless hotspot.

Note: When utilizing this function, you may be subject to additional fees.

- More connection options: adjust settings as needed to manage additional capabilities.

   Note: Depending on the version, not all advertised functions may be included.

Wi-Fi

To use a Wi-Fi network and gain access to the web and other networked devices, turn on the Wi-Fi function.

Connecting to a Wi-Fi network

1. Enable Wi-Fi by going to Connections > Settings > Wi-Fi and tapping the button.

2. Pick a network from the available wireless options.

   Locked networks are those that demand a password to access.

Note: After initially connecting to a Wi-Fi network, your device will automatically reconnect to that network whenever it is in range, without prompting you for a password. Press the network icon, and then press ⚙ > Auto reconnect switch to turn off automatic network connection.

- Restart the wireless router or your device if you are having trouble connecting to a wireless network.

Wi-Fi Direct

With Wi-Fi Direct, no access point is needed to establish a wireless connection between two devices.

1. Enable Wi-Fi by going to Connections > Settings > Wi-Fi and tapping the button.

2. Touch ⋮ > Wi-Fi Direct.

   This page lists the gadgets that have been spotted.

   If the gadget you wish to link up with isn't there, you may always ask it to activate Wi-Fi Direct.

3. Choose a gadget to link up with.

   Once the target device responds positively to the Wi-Fi Direct connection request, the devices will be linked.

Select the device you want to detach from the list and click the Disconnect button.

Bluetooth

Transfer information or media files between Bluetooth-enabled gadgets with the use of Bluetooth.

Precaution: Data transmitted or received by Bluetooth may be susceptible to loss, interception, or misuse, for which Samsung accepts no responsibility.

- Only send and receive information from trustworthy, secure devices at all times. The effective distance between two devices may be diminished if there are physical barriers in their path.

- Your device may not be compatible with some other devices, especially those that have not been certified by the Bluetooth Special Interest Group (SIG).

- Do not make unauthorized copies of files or illegally tap communications for financial gain when using the Bluetooth capability. If you use Bluetooth for illicit purposes, Samsung will not be held liable for any consequences.

Pairing with other Bluetooth devices

1. To turn on Bluetooth, go to the Settings screen and select Connections > Bluetooth. We'll make a list of all the gadgets we find.

2. Pick a gadget to connect with.

   Put it into Bluetooth pairing mode if the device you wish to connect to isn't already on the list. If you need help with the other gadget, see its handbook.

   Note: If you have the Bluetooth settings screen open, other devices can see your device.

3. Grant permission for the gadget to connect through Bluetooth.

   When one device sends out a Bluetooth connection request and the other device accepts it, the two devices will be linked.

Hit the name of the device you want to unpair, and then hit the Unpair button.

Sending and receiving data

These days, Bluetooth data transfer is supported by a wide variety of apps. With other Bluetooth devices, you can exchange information like contacts and media files. The steps below serve as an example of transmitting an image to another gadget.

1. Open Gallery and pick an existing image.

2. Select a receiving device from the list that appears when you tap ⁂ > Bluetooth icon. If the device you wish to pair with isn't listed, you can ask the device's owner to make it visible.

3. Allow the other device to connect to yours through Bluetooth.

Data saver (Mobile network enabled models)

You may limit your data usage by stopping specific apps from sending or receiving data while they are in the background.

To enable data savings, go to Settings > Connections > Data consumption > Data saver.

Data saver feature activated

Note: If you turn on Data saver and then tap Allowed to use data, you'll be able to pick which apps can access data without being throttled.

Mobile data only apps (Mobile network enabled models)

In spite of being connected to a Wi-Fi network, you can tell certain apps to constantly use mobile data.

For apps you want to keep private, or for streaming apps that can be disconnected, you can restrict the device to use only mobile data. The apps will still open utilizing mobile data even if you do not disable Wi-Fi.

Connectivity > Data usage > Mobile data only apps should be enabled in Settings, after which the desired apps' toggles should be flipped.

Note: When utilizing this function, you may be subject to additional fees.

Mobile Hotspot (Mobile network enabled models)

Share your mobile data connection with other devices by setting up your handset as a mobile hotspot.

1. Navigate to Connections > Mobile Hotspot and Tethering > Mobile Hotspot from the Settings screen.

2. The on/off switch needs to be tapped twice.

   There will be a status-icon 🛜 representation of this.

   To modify the password and security settings, select Configure.

3. Locate your gadget in the other gadget's Wi-Fi networks list and tap it to connect. If you like, you may also tap the QR code on the mobile hotspot screen and then use the other device to scan it.

Note: If the mobile hotspot isn't showing up in your device's list of available networks, try switching the band to 2.4 GHz, tapping Advanced, and then tapping the Hidden network option.

More connection settings

You can adjust your settings to manage various aspects of your connection.

Select Connections > More connection settings from the Settings menu.

- Scan for nearby devices to connect to by enabling this feature.

- Printing: Manage the printer add-ons you've installed. To print a document, you can either look for nearby printers or manually add one. For further reading, check out Printing.

- VPN: Connect to a private network at school or work by configuring a virtual private network (VPN) on your device.

- Private DNS: Make use of a private DNS service for more protection on your device.

- Ethernet: A wired network and advanced networking controls are at your fingertips with Ethernet.

Printing

Make changes to the printer's plug-in settings. Images and documents can be printed from the device by linking it to a printer over Wi-Fi or Wi-Fi Direct.

Note: The device might not work with all printers.

Adding printer plugins

Plug in any printers you intend to use with the gadget.

1. Select Connections > More connection settings > Printing > Download plugin from the Settings screen.

2. Download and set up a printer driver.

3. Decide which printer add-on you already have set up.

When you connect to a Wi-Fi network, your device will look for nearby printers automatically.

4. Pick a printer to install.

Note: Select ⋮ > Add printer to add a printer to your list manually.

Printing content

To print images or documents while viewing them, choose Print >▼>All printers... from the content's menu.

Note: The printing process may change based on the material being printed.

Sound

Adjust the device's volume and ringtone settings.

Access the Sound menu from the Settings screen.

- Choose between a "sound" mode and a "silent" mode for your device.

- To temporarily silence your device, you can utilize the "temporary mute" feature.

- Adjust the phone's ringtone here.

- Modify the sound played when a notice is received.

- To change the volume on your device, go to Settings > Volume.

- Alter the tone played when doing specific system tasks like charging.

- Adjust the device's volume and sound effects settings. To learn more about this topic, check out the Sound quality and effects page.

- Set the device so that media sounds from a selected app play independently on the second audio device. For more information, check out Make app sounds discrete.

Note: Depending on the version, not all advertised functions may be included.

Sound quality and effects

Modify the device's audio settings to your liking.

Select Sound > Sound quality and effects from the Settings menu.

- Dolby Atmos lets you choose a surround sound mode that's tailored to different sorts of audio, like movies, music, and speech.

  Dolby Atmos allows you to hear music and sound effects that seem to come from all directions.

- Enjoy the immersive, game-optimized Dolby Atmos soundscape while you play.

Note: Some models require an earphone connection before you may access certain functionalities.

Separate apps sound

You can tell it to play music from a certain app on the Bluetooth speaker or headset you've paired it with.

You can, for instance, play music from the Music app through the car's Bluetooth speaker while listening to the Navigation app on your mobile device.

1. Open the app's settings menu and navigate to Sound > Separate app sound.

2. Use the Back button to go back to the app you just picked to play media sounds independently.

3. Pick an output for the app's media playback.

Notifications

Modify the alert preferences.

In the menu for customization, select Notifications.

- Choose a notification pop-up style and customize the alert's appearance and behavior.

- Under "Recently Sent," you can see which applications have received notifications recently and make adjustments to your notification preferences. Select an app from the applications list and then tap More > ▼ > All to modify its notification settings.

- Do not disturb: Turns off all sounds on the device save for predefined ones.

- You can adjust more granular settings for alerts under the "Advanced" tab.

Display

Modify how the screen looks and how you get around the Home screen.

Select Display from the Settings menu.

- Light/Dark: Switch between light and dark modes here.

- Dark mode settings: When using the device at night or in a dimly lit room, you can lessen the strain on your eyes by activating the dark mode settings. Dark mode can be activated on a timer that you specify.

  Note: Some programs may be unable to utilize the dark mode.

- Brightness: The brightness control allows you to fine-tune the screen's luminance.

- Adaptive brightness enables the device to remember your brightness settings and apply them automatically in future situations where the lighting is the same or very similar.

- Eye comfort shield: Reduce eye strain with the help of the "Eye Comfort Shield," which filters out some of the blue light from your screen. This function can be applied on a timed basis that you specify.

- Font size and style: Make adjustments to the font size and style.

- Screen zoom: Adjust the size of everything on the screen with the zoom feature.

- Screen timeout: Timeout settings for the screen allow you to control when the screen goes dark after inactivity.

- Edge panels: Edge panels' configurations can be modified.

- Navigation bar: Modify the options for the navigation bar.

- Screen saver: You can put the smartphone to sleep while it charges by activating a screen saver.

Note: Depending on the version, not all advertised functions may be included.

Wallpaper

Alter the background images used in the Home and locked screens. Select Wallpaper from the Settings menu.

Home screen

Alter the Home screen's settings, like its appearance.

Select Home screen from the Settings menu

Lock screen

Make some adjustments to the locked screen options.

Select Lock screen from the Settings menu.

- There's a toggle for changing how the screen locks.

- Smart Lock allows you to program your device to unlock automatically when it senses certain trusted places or objects.

- Secure lock settings: Adjust the safety lock parameters for the currently active lock method.

- Wallpaper services: enable wallpaper services like Dynamic Lock screen on your device.

- Clock style: The locked screen's clock can have its font and color customized.

- Roaming clock: set the locked screen's clock to display both the current time and the user's home time zone.

- Widgets: Modify the widgets on the locked screen to suit your needs.

- Contact information: Your email address and other contact information might be displayed on the locked screen of your device.

- Notifications: Manage how alerts appear while the screen is locked.

- Choose apps to get quick access icons for them on the locked screen.

- View the Lock screen version and legal information under "About Lock screen."

Note: Depending on the manner of locking the screen, several customization choices may be made available.

Smart Lock

The gadget can be programmed to unlock and remain unlocked when it detects certain people, places, or things that you designate as trusted.

You can set up your home as a trusted location, and when you return there, your device will unlock itself.

To set up a Smart Lock, go to the Settings screen and then hit Lock screen > Smart Lock.

Note: After deciding on a screen lock technique, you'll be able to use this function.

- The screen will lock after four hours of inactivity, and you'll need your pattern, PIN, or password to unlock it.

Chapter Six
Biometrics and security

Adjust the device's security settings as needed.

Click on Biometrics and security in the Settings area.

- Face recognition: You can use the device's facial recognition features to unlock the screen with just a glance.

- More biometrics settings: tailor your system's behavior based on your biometric data. The biometrics security patch's version can be viewed, and updates can be checked for.

- Google play protect: Set your smartphone to scan for malicious software and behavior with Google Play Protect, get alerts if anything looks suspicious, then delete or report it.

- Security update: check the firmware version and install any available patches.

- Google play system update: You may see the current version of the Google Play system and see whether there are any updates available.

- Find My Mobile: You can switch on/off the Find My Mobile feature here. To locate and manage a misplaced Samsung device, visit the Find My Mobile webpage (findmymobile.samsung.com).

- To install programs from an unknown source, you must first enable this feature.

- Encrypt SD card: To protect data stored on an SD card, you can configure your device to do so.

  Precaution: With this option activated, your device will be unable to decrypt your files even if you restore it to factory settings. Before performing a factory reset, disable this option.

- Other security settings: Additional safeguards can be established under the Other Security Settings menu item.

Note: Depending on your service provider or device model, some features may be disabled.

Face recognition

The device can be programmed to unlock itself upon recognizing the user's face.

Note: If you set up facial recognition as a screen lock, it won't work the first time you power on the device. A pattern, PIN, or password you create while registering your face is required to access the device's interface. Make sure you don't lose track of your password, PIN, or pattern.

- Swipe and None are insecure screen lock options that will erase all biometric information. You'll need to re-register your biometric information every time you utilize a new app or function that requires it.

Precautions for using face recognition

Keep these things in mind before you try using face recognition to unlock your iPhone.

- A person or thing that closely resembles your image may be able to unlock your device.

- Compared to using a pattern, PIN, or password, facial recognition lacks security.

For better face recognition
Think about these things before employing facial recognition:

- Registration under these circumstances may be delayed if you wear glasses, a hat, a mask, a beard, or a lot of cosmetics.

- Better match results can be achieved by registering in a well-lit area with a clean camera lens.

- Ensuring that your image is clear and focused

Registering your face
Avoid registering your face in bright sunshine by doing so indoors.

1. Select Biometrics and security > Face recognition from the Settings menu.

2. Follow the on-screen prompts and click Continue.

3. Lock the screen in place.

4. Bring your head into viewable area of the screen. Your face will be scanned by the camera.

Note: If your face isn't being recognized during the unlock process, you can reset it by tapping Remove face data.

Unlocking the screen with your face

In place of a pattern, PIN, or password, you can just use your face to unlock the screen.

1. Select Biometrics and security Face recognition from the Settings menu.

2. Activate the previously established screen lock system.

3. Press the Face unlock button to begin using it.

4. Check the locked screen by looking at it.

   Facial recognition allows you to bypass the need for a password or other security measure.

   Use the factory default method of locking the screen if your face is not recognized.

Deleting the registered face data

Your facial recognition data can be removed at any time.

1. Select Biometrics and security Face recognition from the Settings menu.

2. Activate the previously established screen lock system.

3. Face data can be deleted with three taps.

   If a face is registered and then removed, any features that rely on it will likewise be disabled.

Privacy

Make the necessary privacy adjustments.

Select Privacy from the Settings menu.

- Permission manager: The Permission Manager allows you to see which programs have access to which functionalities. The security settings can also be modified.

- Samsung: Customization Service settings and other account related information can be managed at Samsung.com.

- Google recommends adjusting your privacy settings to the highest level.

Note: Depending on your service provider or device model, some features may be disabled.

Location

Modify the permissions for accessing location data.

Select Location in the Settings menu.

- App permission: See which ones can use your location and change that setting if necessary.

- Improve accuracy: If you want more precise location data even when the Wi-Fi or Bluetooth is turned off, you can boost the device's accuracy by changing the settings.

- Recent location requests: You can see which apps have recently asked for your location by tapping on the "Recent location requests" option.

- Location service: The device's location services can be viewed.

Google

Adjust the preferences for Google services. Google may be accessed through the Settings menu.

Account and backup

Use Samsung Cloud to sync, back up, or recover your device's data. Smart Switch also allows you to sign in to your Samsung account or your Google account, as well as move data to and from other devices.

Click on Accounts and backup in the Settings area.

- Sync your Samsung and Google accounts, or any others, by going to Settings > Accounts.

- Users: Create new user accounts so that others can use your device with their own unique settings (email, background, etc.). For more information, see Users.

  Note: It's possible that this function is unavailable in your area or through your service provider.

- Samsung Cloud: With Samsung Cloud, you can back up your information and settings, and even if you lose your old device, you can get back to where you were.

- Google Drive: Use Google Drive to back up all of your important files, documents, and app settings. Your private data can be backed up. In order to back up data, you must be logged into your Google account.

- Smart Switch: Launch Smart Switch to move information from your old device. For additional information about Smart Switch, see Switching from an Old Device.

Note: Always keep a copy of your data offsite, whether it's on Samsung Cloud or your PC, in case anything happens to your device and you need to perform a factory data reset.

Users

Create new user profiles so that other people who will be using the device can each have their own email, wallpaper, and other settings.

Note: It's possible that this function is unavailable in your area or through your service provider.

Available user accounts fall into the following categories:

- Administrator: The administrator account can only be created once during the initial setup of the device. This account can manage all other accounts on the device. Only from this account can new users be created or existing ones deleted.

- Guests can use the device with the Guest account. Guests have access to temporary storage for any data or information utilized during their session. Every time you log in with this account, you'll be given the option to either continue your previous session or start fresh.

- Users can access their own apps and material, as well as change system-wide settings, by creating a "new user" account.

- New restricted account: For example, the new restricted account cannot access any services that need a login other than those explicitly granted by the administrator account. (Wi-Fi versions).

Adding users

1. Select Users from the Accounts and backup menu in the Settings menu.

2. Follow the on-screen prompts to create a new user account by selecting the "Add user" or "Add user or profile" option.

Adding restricted profiles (Wi-Fi models)

1. Select Users from the Accounts and backup menu in the Settings menu.

2. Follow the on screen prompts to create a new user account by tapping "Add user or profile" and then "User (limited profile).

Switching users

To switch to a different account, tap the user icon that appears at the top of the locked screen.

Locked screen

Managing users

The administrator has the ability to modify or remove user accounts as needed.

Accounts and backup > Users can be accessed from the Settings menu.

Select the user whose account you wish to delete, then select Delete user.

Access your account's configuration menu by selecting "User Account" from the menu.

Samsung Cloud

Store your data in Samsung Cloud and access it from any other device.

Backing up data

Samsung Cloud can be used to create backups of your device's data.

1. Select Samsung Cloud and then select Back up data on the Settings screen.

2. Choose the boxes next to the files you wish to save and then select Back up now.

3. Hit Done when you finish

Note: Some information will not be saved in a backup. On the Settings screen, select Accounts and backup, then touch Back up data under Samsung Cloud to view the specifics of the data that will be stored up.

- From the Settings screen, click Accounts and backup > Restore data > a device to access its backup data in your Samsung Cloud.

Restoring data

Samsung Cloud allows you to restore your device's backup from the cloud.

1. Select Accounts and backup from the Settings menu.

2. Choose a device from the list, and then tap the Restore data button. Three, select the files you wish to recover and then click the recover button.

Advanced features

Turn on complex functions and adjust their configurations.

To access these, select Advanced features from the Settings screen.

- Make and receive calls and send and receive texts from any of your other Samsung-enabled devices.

- If you have an Android device and a compatible car, you may use Android Auto to access select functions of your phone right from the dashboard.

- Modify your Quick Share preferences here: Quick Share. For more, check out Quick Share.

- Use experimental software or hardware.

- Choose an app or function to activate with the Side key.

- Gestures and motions: Turn on the motion feature and adjust the preferences. For more, read up on some hand motions and facial expressions.

- Modify the capture settings for screenshots and screen recording.

- Contacts displayed when sharing: This feature allows you to see who you've been in touch with on the sharing choices box.

- Accessories: Modify how your gadgets interact with the system.

- Launch the game using the "Game Launcher" option. For more information on Game Launcher, go here.

Note: Depending on your service provider or device model, some features may be disabled.

Motions and gestures

Turn on the motion sensor and adjust the parameters.

Select Motions and gestures under Advanced features in Settings.

- If the screen is off and you double-tap anyplace on it, you can tell the device to turn on the screen.

- Double-tapping an empty spot on the Home screen or the locked screen will cause the screen to turn off.

- By covering the screen, you can silence the gadget or select noises.

- If you want to take a screenshot with a palm swipe, you can configure your smartphone to do so. Gallery is where you may check out the snapped pics. Some programs and functions prevent you from taking a screenshot.

Note: Some sensor-based functionality may get an unexpected input if the device is shaken or dropped excessively.

Digital wellbeing and parental controls

Examine your device's activity log and implement security settings to stop it from disrupting your life. You can manage your kids' digital time by setting up parental controls.

Select Digital Wellbeing and parental controls from the Settings menu.

- Screen time: Limiting daily screen time is important, so make it one of your goals.

- App timers: establish a daily limit for how long you can spend on each app. Once you've used up your allotted time, the app will no longer function.

- Focus mode: Switch on focus mode to keep from being sidetracked by your gadget. In this mode, you can access just the apps that you already authorized.

- Bedtime mode: If you suffer from eye strain when trying to fall asleep, turning on bedtime mode may help.

- Driving monitor: Turn on the driving monitor to keep track of how much time you spend using your phone while behind the wheel.

- Parental controls: Take charge of your kids' screen time with the help of parental controls.

Chapter Seven
Battery and device care

You can check in on the health of your battery, storage, memory, and security settings with the device care tool. Automatic optimization of the gadget is also a click away.

Optimizing your device

Battery and device care Optimize now can be found in the Settings menu.

The following are the steps taken by the fast optimization feature to enhance device performance.

- To end any background processes or applications.
- Taking care of abnormal battery consumption
- Checking for corrupted software and malicious code.

Using the auto optimization feature

When your gadget isn't in use, you can have it automatically optimize itself. Just flip the switch under Automation, then Auto-Optimize Daily. Select Time to schedule automatic optimization.

Battery

See how much juice your gadget still has left. If your device's battery is low, turn on power saving mode to extend its life.

Navigate to Battery and device maintenance Battery on the Settings screen.

- To get most use out of your battery life, turn on power saving mode.

- Apps you don't regularly use can have their background power consumption capped.

- Extra battery options: tweak the battery's more complex settings.

Note: The remaining battery life is displayed in the usage time left field. Your device's remaining usage time may be different based on its current settings and conditions.

- Some apps in power saving mode may stop sending you notifications.

Storage

Find out how much memory is being utilized and how much is still free.

Battery and device care > Storage can be found in the Settings menu. Choose a folder from which you want to remove files or software that you no longer need. Next, choose an item by tapping and holding on it, and then press Delete or Uninstall.

Note: Since the operating system and preinstalled apps take up some space in internal memory, the real accessible capacity is less than the stated capacity. When you update your device, its storage options could shift.

- Internal storage space may be seen in the Samsung website's Specifications for your device.

Memory

Battery and device maintenance > Memory may be found in the Settings menu.

Select the apps you want to remove from the list and then hit Clean now to have them removed from background processing and speed up your smartphone.

Device protection

Verify the device's current level of protection. Anti-malware scanning is performed by this function.

Select Battery and device maintenance > Device protection > Scan tablet from the Settings menu.

Apps

Control and customize the device's installed software. You may examine app data, modify app permissions and notifications, and delete or disable unused software.

Click the Apps button in the Settings menu.

General management

Modify the system settings or factory reset your smartphone.

Select General administration from the Settings menu.

- Language: Select the language you'd like your device to use.

- Text to speech output: Modify the language, speaking rate, and other parameters of the text-to-speech output utilized by Talkback.

- Time and date: View and adjust options for customizing the device's time and date display.

  Note: The time and date are reset if the battery is completely depleted.

- Samsung keyboard settings: To modify the Samsung keyboard's settings, go to the keyboard's "Settings" menu.

- Change the default keyboard and view a list of available keyboards in the "Keyboard list and default" section.

- Physical keyboard: You can adjust the settings for a physical keyboard.

- Mouse and track pad: If you're using a mouse or trackpad, you can adjust their settings here.

- Auto fill service: Pick an auto fill service from the available options.

- Reset: You can return your smartphone to its factory settings by pressing the "Reset" button.

- Contact us: Post a query or check out the F.A.Q.

Adding device languages

Your device supports the addition of additional languages.

1. To add a new language, select it from the General management section of the Settings menu. Select ⋮ >All Languages to see a list of available translations.

2. Pick a second language

3. By tapping the **Set as default** button, you can make the current language the default. Select **Keep current** to retain the currently selected language.

The chosen tongue will be added to your existing linguistic repertoire. The language you choose as the default will be prioritized in the list.

If you wish to make a different language your system's default, choose it from the list and then hit the Apply button. The next supported language will be utilized if a program does not support the default language.

Accessibility

Adjust the parameters to make the gadget more user-friendly.

Select Accessibility from the Settings menu.

- Check out the accessibility options you're already using and learn about additional options we think you'll find helpful.

- To hear feedback through your device's speaker, activate TalkBack. Select Settings Tutorial and help to see how to utilize this function.

- Visibility improvements: adjust the settings to make the app more usable for people with visual impairments.

- Accessibility settings can be adjusted to better accommodate users with hearing loss.

- Interaction and dexterity: Adjust the parameters to make the app more usable for people with limited finger or hand mobility.

- The "Advanced" tab is where you may adjust things like Direct access and notifications.

- Accessibility features already installed on your device can be viewed in the "Installed Services" menu.

- Check out the Accessibility details if you want to know more.

- Contact us: Post a query or check out the F.A.Q.

Software update

Using the firmware over-the-air (FOTA) service, you can update your device's software remotely. Software upgrades can be pre-scheduled as well.

Choose Software update from the menu under Settings.

- Download and set up: manually check for and set up updates.

- When connected to a Wi-Fi network, the device can be programmed to automatically download updates via the "Auto download over Wi-Fi" setting.

- Click "Last Update" to see when the software was last updated.

Note: In the event that critical security upgrades are issued, they will be installed on your device without your knowledge or consent.

Security updates information

The purpose of these updates is to improve your device's security so that you and your data are safer. Visit security.samsungmobile.com for the latest updates specific to your model's security.

Remote support

The remote support service is there to assist you in the event that you have any technical inquiries or issues with your equipment.

Select Remote help from the Settings menu.